STUBBORN

STUBBORN

Jean Gallagher

Oberlin College Press
Oberlin, Ohio

The following poems, some under different titles, have appeared in: *Barrow Street*: "Nativity," "Show Me"; *Commonweal*: "Particular Annunciation," "Spin, " "Two Sermons," "Annunciation/Expulsion," "Early Photograph I," "What Now"; *The Journal* (Ohio State University): "Stubborn," "No Place But"; *Margie: The American Journal of Poetry*: "How Many," "Detail of Paradise"; *Notre Dame Review*: "*Annuncio di morte a Maria*," "A Short Film About the New Math"; *Rhino*: "Early Photograph II."

The FIELD Poetry Series, vol. 19

Oberlin College Press, 50 N. Professor Street, Oberlin, OH 44074

www.oberlin.edu/ocpress

Cover and book design: Steve Farkas

Library of Congress Cataloging-in-Publication Data

Gallagher, Jean, 1962–
 Stubborn / Jean Gallagher.
   p. cm. — (The Field poetry series ; v. 19)
   ISBN 0-932440-27-4 (pbk. : alk. paper)
   I. Title. II. Series.
   PS3607.A415434S78   2006
   811'.6—dc22   2006004403

As ever, for the teachers of a stubborn mind:

Marie Ponsot
Janet Abels
and
David Birdsell

Contents

Part I: Story in Five Annunciations

Part II: A Short Film About the New Math

Part III: Catherine Cycle

Part IV: Stubborn

Part I

Story in Five Annunciations

Particular Annunciation

(Fra Angelico, *Annunciation*, ca. 1449)

The thought arrives like Gabriel with its
art deco wings, sleek as glazed porcelain,
striped and full of eyes as a hallucination,
not seeming suited for flight: *I could do it.*

In the particular annunciation
she and the angel bow politely, hands
crossed flat over flat chests: two businessmen
in gracious, wary negotiation.
Neither speaks. She is blank as a drum,
poker-faced. But the open porch
where they incline toward each other hums
like a force field. Framed in her separate arch,
the speckled, burnished light around her head hovers,
contained but expandable, and says, *think it over.*

Annunciation/Expulsion

(Giovanni di Paolo, ca. 1440)

Inside, the house opened like a doll's,
the done deal is just starting to settle

over the leaning-toward and -away
of arched walls, lily, her averted, attentive face.

Outside, the future is blowing
its gold hurricane. They are crossing

out of their companioned solitude among the animals,
the intelligent, upstanding rabbits and red, edible

flowers, their feet curving carpet needles
in the blue-green domestic grasses

they are turning to leave. Crossing into *next*,
its gravities, necessities, haphazard plots.

Annuncio di morte a Maria

(Duccio, ca. 1308)

It all looks familiar   the still open book   the adjoining
                    rooms reeling back into nowhere   the once dazzling
         visitor crowding the doorway   making offers   keeping his distance.

But her color is   well   green   as if
                    she's just been fished up from the too late.
         Even the visitor looks bleached by this one last trip into voice.

But the news is not ever what you think it is.
                    The news is not what you think.

Here   here is the other lily   stripped down to its central cluster of sparks.
                    Here is the other hovering bright idea.

Giacometti's *Cage (Woman and Head)* as Annunciation

I saw you coming a long way off inside my eye:
little flicker of wings
I built this high room for.
Now you have the stubborn mass of all big ideas,
welded to the spot like some terrible sofa
always behind my back.
What do I do with you now that I know
the walls are as soft as oxygen?
I'm like Rapunzel up here and what are you?
The golden hair, the straw I'm burning.

Annunciation Suspended

And what if she remains uninterrupted
by the spectacular descent   the difficult
worthy agenda?
                              Just this room's
regular breathing filling with   emptying light.
The book opens in her attention until
it is the room she breathes in.   Hers the only
heartbeat here   the secret life   the secret life.

Part II

A Short Film About the New Math

Spin

(Bicci di Lorenzo, *St. Nicholas Providing Dowries to Three Virgins*, 1433)

He gives a push with one foot and sets
the room spinning. Coins just bearing
      the weightless, inflated expense of the possible

float like empty gold planets over
the bed's red continent. The girls spin
      inside their lives, all their luck reversible

until this hour's gears re-engage
and the stories put in motion take on
      their increasingly plausible, unforeseeable freight.

A Short Film About the New Math

(Giotto, *Noli Me Tangere*, ca. 1315)

Hemmed in by shining unreal numbers
I'm the only thing here with an assignable value.
I just want something to put my hands on
not this exhausting country of calculation and light
its spotless silent machinery   all flight and clean exits.

Nothing is where I left it   not even
the weighty bloody ending I took down and buried
like a faithful dog with the very last bone.
I came back to smudge my fingerprints on the wreckage
and what do I find instead   a pristine early matinee
in a perfect foreign language and no subtitles
a transparency written over
with a faultless differential calculus
I'll never be able to grasp.

Mathematician   mineral star
before the film stock
of the present tense
dissolves completely
into your weightless
imaginary integers
take off your gold gloves and fight me
take off your gold mask and kiss.

Two Sermons

(Workshop of Giotto, *St. Francis Preaching to the Birds*,
ca. 1300)

Birds drop like consonants and vowels
from a single tree, array themselves in
alphabetic ranks that spell the sermon
back to him. Omnilect and legible,
he speed-reads light as speech empties
into it. He leans, treelike, and reaches
into what's reading him out loud: the weightless
shine between the denser flying syllables.
The old fixed polar stars, transmitter
and receiver, fade in his attention's
pure gold nowhere. Behind him, his brother
monk signals in their shared, resistant
language the more usable solid fictions,
no realer than this but more insistent.

How Many

(Sassetta, *St. Thomas Aquinas in Prayer*, ca. 1427)

Silence is simultaneous
departure arrival

what am I leaving
what leaning into

God is the doorway
I keep walking through

how many places
are there to hide here

how many ways to be found

Detail of Paradise

(Giovanni di Paolo, ca. 1440)

Particularity evidently survives in paradise.
Your own uniform, the modesty of it, still fits.
Your bruises and cuts still glimmer.
The goldapple trees still stand up like the very first numbers you ever learned,
and love's sentence—*I am so glad you're here*—is still what you say.

Part III

Catherine Cycle

Catherine Cycle

(Giovanni di Paolo, ca. 1460)

Catherine of Siena (1347-1380), the twenty-third of twenty-five children in a prosperous family, was a lay member of the Dominican order who devoted her life to the care of the sick, mysticism, preaching, and church politics. She acquired a sizeable number of followers during her lifetime, and was the subject of an even larger cult after her death, primarily because of her mystical experiences: trances in which she claimed to participate in direct dialogues with God, to have married Christ, and to have received stigmata. She could read but did not learn to write until she was thirty; most of her letters, spontaneous prayers, and her reports of her trance experiences were dictated to secretaries in her native Sienese dialect, although she evidently knew Latin. She corresponded and had frequent audience with church leaders, advising and berating them on matters of church reform. Much of what we know about her life comes from Raymond of Capua, her confessor, spiritual advisor, secretary, translator, and first biographer. Using Raymond's biography as his source, Giovanni di Paolo painted a cycle of Catherine's life around the time of her canonization.

I. Mysterious Communion

Catherine of Siena miraculously receives communion from
Christ while her confessor, officiating in another chapel in the
church, raises his hand in astonishment at the consecrated
wafer, from which a piece has disappeared.
—Metropolitan Museum of Art, New York

It is always something happening in the other room.
Bright sliver of here
suddenly missing
lost packet of light
swallowed into elsewhere.
I'm holding the empty place
I'm holding the empty place open
as she pokes her finger through the black ice of time
puts her hands in the gold mess
lets it burn down her arms like honey.
All the clocks slow down keep slowing.
I try to keep an eye on her
but what I see is visible husk
trace of her exit her entrance
past the edge of events.

II. Exchange

(Catherine ascends in rapture over the rooftops of Siena and exchanges her heart with Christ's. Meanwhile, Raymond considers the etymology of her name.)

Catherine comes from catha, *which means total, and* ruina, *ruin; hence "total ruin." . . . Or Catherine's name may be taken from* catenula, *a small chain.*
                    —Jacobus de Voragine, *The Golden Legend*, 1260

Utter ruin
little chain.
Heartblood litters the rooftops.
In my dreams I clank along behind her
slam against the housewalls
catch my feet in the gutters.
What she has broken apart in me keeps rattling.
She doesn't bother to ask anymore
Did you see that?
No argument.
Just a look in her eyes like frozen milk
I know not to ask questions.

III. Her Marriage

I look like I am standing still don't I
a singularity in a white dress
as space opens away from me like a dancefloor.
But I can tell you I marry everything
down to the last gold atom.
Marry is you may have guessed a placeholder verb
wedding picture a circuit-breaker
until you can see fast enough
to follow the electric road of my touch
lighting every halo along the way.

IV. Dictation

Something burning right through
the wall's gold leaf.
Sounds   who hears them.
This listening a stellar furnace
where the pristine hydrogen of just one word
fuses into the bluish helium alphabet
sodium verbs carbon syntax iron vulgate I heard
inside my mother's twenty-third birth.
I can handle these elements   can you catch them.

V. Stigmata

What I want
and therefore am not
beats in my chest   trapped bird.
Desire says open the skin.

VI. Her Mother

(Catherine's mother dies unrepentent; Catherine prays for another chance.)

There's a lot I can stand and even welcome
the five kinds of tears including fire
all the roaring nothing that fills my room
but not the eternal wreck she's made.
How hard do I need to push
to spin this wheel backward
just a turn or two   just enough
to slit open what she has sewn shut
to retie the minute she's snapped off
like a red thread between her teeth.

VII. With the Pope and the College of Cardinals

She rebuked the Pope and all his cardinals with such a constant boldness for their base minds and lack of manly courage in God's course, that they were all forced to confess that it was not she that spake, but the spirit and wisdom of God in her.

* * *

I have made every effort, insofar as is allowed by the Latin syntax, to translate word for word, though strictly speaking this cannot always be done without adding some kind of interpolation, a conjunction or an adverb for instance, that is not in the original.

—Raymond of Capua

My throat a high road
where two voices signal and pass each other
which one arrives first don't ask me.
Look at their faces like bronze church doors
closing.
Raymond taking notes   I'd like to see those later
before they're immersed in the alchemical bleach
of his perfect Latin.
He insists on conjunctions adverbs
keeps asking *how? connected how?*
I just tell him what you told me
open the ear of your desire.
This voice no matter whose
winds around their red hats
a mercury scarf they can't untie
coats the walls like a sulfur encaustic
they'll never quite figure out how to scrape off.

VIII. Her Death

This is where   listening becomes its sounds
This is where   there's only world
This is where   you've never left
This is where   nothing keeps
                    itself

Part IV

Stubborn

Stubborn

(Duccio, *Maestà* Altarpiece, 1308-1311)

The Maestà *panel appears to fulfill a very concrete function. It illustrates in biblical sequence the events that continually occupied the spiritual eye of Mary during her meditations before her assumption into heaven. To the medieval urban viewer, who in general would not have been able to undertake a pilgrimage to the* loca sancta, *this sequence of images appeared as a vehicle for an alternative, imaginary pilgrimage to these sites. In this way viewers could replicate the actual meditative practice of Mary in Jerusalem.*

—Peter Seiler, "Duccio's *Maestà*"

I. Front, Central Panel

Slide

(Virgin Enthroned with Child, Angels, Saints)

Everyone carries a little something
reminder   what I was   what I did there
      my heart's first name.

        Mine is the baby
the loss machine
      the primitive camera that sucked in light like milk.

    I hold the slides up to the light.   Everyone leans in to see.   That was me
enthroned in the visible world's gold minute.   Whose heart spins
    the engine in the slide projector.   When it stops spinning   who will know.

II. Front, Predella

Nativity

Radium stopwatch   out of my pocket
breathes on its own like a great idea.
How does it work   the angels of attention keep asking.
Attention's animals ask   *what next.*

Show Me

(*Epiphany* and *Presentation in the Temple*)

*And Simeon blessed them, and said unto Mary . . . , Yea, a
sword shall pierce through thy own soul also, that the thoughts
of many hearts may be revealed.*

—Luke 2:35

Everything's bitter shiny gifts pile up
at the door. In my lap the grenade
with the pin out. *Oh yes you too will have your heart
that red glass window broken. How else to meet
yourself   scattered and identical everywhere like snow.*

Lucky

(Flight into Egypt)

The dream says *there is a place to hide.*
But we never drop the little problem you named
Going-Going-Gone. Led by the angel
What-Did-You-Expect. The angel Look-
the-Other-Way. Lucky for you your dreamlife
is so real. Oh love, lucky for us.

Just a Moment Please

(Massacre of the Innocents)

Time hits the room in helicopter blades   what I love
goes down like grass.   *Wait*   I say   leaning
just a little out of grief's gravity well.   *Just*
a moment please.   My loss turns   looks straight
at me.   *Yes?*   it says.   The things I want
to ask it silt up like blood   like happiness
in my mouth.   My life has always
flickered like the light between the blades.

III. Reverse, Predella

Early Photograph I

(Temptation on the Pinnacle of the Temple)

Here's one of me up on hunger's
        balcony, my head just emerging

from the gold smog of childhood, my ideas
        still stuck to my back like new wings.

Oh the trouble they gave me on the way
        down, not because they didn't open

but because they did, catching on all
        the invisible, simple machinery of the air,

all I had to trust to when I cast
        myself down into my life, jumped away

from the shadow-parent, the formal exams, the temptation
        to stay suspended in perfect thirst forever.

Early Photograph II

(Temptation on the Mountain)

What you don't see here is how I was *always* dragging
myself out of the wilderness, every five minutes
or so, for years at a time. My mind never
tired of its uranium tricks, the lead
and carbon, the black dust stopping up all the vents.
When I finally coughed, the angels clapped.
But it took forever to learn that whatever I wanted,
and I mean *whatever*—bread, power,
the expensive thrill of throwing myself away—
was always already coating my hands, the dust
of a million exploded lightbulbs, a million crushed ideas.

What Now

(Calling of Apostles Peter and Andrew)

You're right in the middle of your life,
a boat on open water green and lively as moss.
It feels like wealth, this floating kingdom,
the nets you've made that fit your hands,
the rustle of *something more, maybe*
in the transparent time around your feet.

But the future is jagging along peripheral vision's sharp coastline.
Its thunder is gilding your ears with something you don't think you've heard before.
Oh no.
What now.
Listening's empty cup is filling and filling with the sound of your name
rhyming with everything else.

OK, so the fish were just an idea you had,
the roughest of sketches, really.
And yet you were sure that they weighed something;
your back still hurt when you hauled them in.

Everything You Know About Water

(*Wedding at Cana*)

It's like every party I've ever forgotten until she says
they have no wine   the way you'd point to the desert and say
*there is no water   now what
are you going to do about that.*

The red thing that breaks loose in my head   *what have I
to do with thee*   bright and tricky
as a bloodclot   *my hour is not
yet come*   I think is just my stubborn love
for things as they seem
the distinctions   the gleaming
separate islands I dreamed
of *I* and *thee* and *hour*.

I fill up the jars with what I always have too much of   my
particular choosy thirst. As they fill
they sound like something she might whisper in my ear

> *Pour out everything
> you know about water
> a transparent glove
> turning inside out
> flashing the red silk lining.*

What did you think weddings were for she says.
Push aside the molecules and drink.

Blind Man Sees

Light breaks me down with its hammers.
Its leprosy rusts me away until even

a dog can see clear through. No going
back now light leaves its bootprints

on my closed eyes. Who even recognizes me
now? I keep saying *it's me it's still me*

but what am I tied now to everything
by sight's glamorous implausible chains?

Progressive Simplification at the Well

(Woman from Samaria)

My children are dead   are grown   were never born.
I have no husband   just a stay-at-home love
that drinks whatever I bring.
You could say I am free but
for the weight of theory   a red jar I fill and fill.

The water he is selling what does it weigh
how much would I have to spill out to buy it?

I dip my finger in the nothing he has to carry
see the sudden transparency
of all I ever did.

Apostles' Dreams I

(Transfiguration of Christ)

The human mask, the temporal sweetness, came off
with a clatter and underneath, well, what else:

light, lots of it, the kind that sends your eyes
skittering in their poor sockets, your teeth screaming

at the root. Oh man, that light came down
like a hammer on the gong of the entire sky,

and there I was, flat out on the ground, stuttering
something about *permanent housing, fireproof walls.*

Forget it, the light said, *we have other plans
for you: listen like the fire eating your life whole.*

Big Door

(Raising of Lazarus)

Why didn't you you could have if only you had
then this wouldn't   Faith is the silver fish-hook
I had to tear out   I called you and called you and
covered the gash with a rock.
Don't move it   I'm asking you   but I can hear
the minutes ripping right along their seams.
Is that my voice   the big door
in my chest screeching open
the stink   all my dead
toxic darlings that look so much like me.
Unbind them   is that what you just said
and let them go free.

IV. Reverse, Central Panel

No Place But

(Entry into Jerusalem)

There is no place but this sharp edge
riding the animal present tense.

No plot; just light's saturated solution.
Just the clear nothing of praise. Just

the under-pigment story scrapes down to
when we meet ourselves suddenly all at once.

The imagined city spills down toward the life
that I am always entering

that I am laying down and taking up
like red clothes and broken branches

in the road built every second
by this patient unstoppable gait.

Self-Diagnosis

(Last Supper)

Lined up all my cells at the table and said:
one of you will. *Which one which one not me*:
little birds, the weight of the early elements,
falling off the high wire into
doubt's life-long, unresisting blue.

Apostles' Dreams II

(John Asleep at the Last Supper)

If they ask you, "What is the evidence of your father in you?"
say to them, "It is motion and rest."
                                                    —*Gospel of Thomas*

In my sleep I hear something turn over
becoming nothing but itself.
What a surprise   all along   just the traffic
of rest and motion. *Rest*
in this I dream him saying
there's nothing to do
with the body but give it.

Apostles' Dreams III

(Jesus Prays on the Mount of Olives)

He walks uphill out of everybody's sleep
turning like a weathervane in the mineral air.
Watch   he says   but what is there to watch
except his drilling down into the granite
of what he already knows?
His solitude weighs too much
for us to hold up   is too hard
to wake into.

Please   is a flag shredding in the sharp gold wind
if you could   a pulse disappearing in the mountain's skull
but if not   the remaining crystal in his blood dissolving
all right   the door between ice and water
                      water and where is it
                      swinging   open   shut   open   open.

Five Views of the Fire

(*Seizure of Jesus*)

1. Bystander Bleeding
(Onlooker Attacked by Angry Adherent of Accused)

I live on the edge of the disaster   I never drink
the water   the schools are never open   there are just
the prickly fences the soldiers put up with their thoughts.
But my life has grown up here somehow   like a tree right out of rock
and even if I lose the ear cut off by love's bafflement
I can still hear you sighing and it sounds like a fire
no one has yet figured how to put out.

2. Little Knife
(Adherent Seeks Outlet)

All I want is to reach
into the hour's furnace and pull
him out. All I have
is the sharp little knife
of wish. Cut a hole
and pour out the fire
that pools in anybody's head.

3. Without
(Adherents Flee)

The punctuation at the end
of the sentence burns off
and we run   we run out
of the language like water
we are no longer
what we thought
we are without

4. Phone Call

(Giveaway Not What I Expected, Says Go-Between)

Yes I was afraid   of your suffocating
house   the glare   no hedge against love's
greater depredations.   No I don't think I meant to burn
the whole thing down.   But what was left
on the cleared ground   I didn't know
I wanted   the kiss entirely
freed   of the weight of future.

5. Thirst

(Accused Delivers Statement, Self)

The torches eat all the water with their
red voices. I can see the road and it only
gets hotter   bruised gold by too much light
and I am already thirsty.   But the present tense
burns cool and impersonal   like a kiss
from nowhere   like the traitorous relief
of putting myself in the hands that give me
away   opened like a box   everything rains
into me now   why am I still thirsty.

Stubborn

(Peter's First Denial)

What happened that time on the water was   out of nothing
more substantial than love   I unweighed myself

and the water forgot me   and I walked.   Disappeared
into the hydrogen-oxygen footsteps and only

started sinking when I thought out loud *but I*
am something else again.   I am something

else.   How stubborn   the idea of a cell that can be
locked.   How busy   all the antibodies

putting up their fences.   He is the virus of myself
and I want him out   the one who named me after

every hard place that will one day
be dissolved   just not yet.

Whatever You Say

(Interrogation by Pilate)

I have my ideas   the gold wreath
around my head   each leaf
a sharp word   *what is the truth*
falling into   gravity's mouth
your silence   eats the air
before I can ask   *where are you from*
you have already gone nowhere completely.

Any Idea

(Crown of Thorns)

Let's face it: how much easier to love what disappears
into idea, a sweet gold smoke
clearing off, leaving just the delicious
lightheadedness of belief. But you are the stubborn, homely
animal in the middle of the only road; the scratchy
gold sweater that's all I have to wear.
Do you have any idea how tiring a chronic
physical god is, how it permeates everything
like a red glue, stopping up the spaces
of sleep, holding together even the trashy
crown I wove from my life's old wires
and metal scraps: all I can offer in exchange
for your ubiquitous needle, unerring thread.

Progress

(Road to Calvary)

The road runs right through the hour's
gleaming centrifuge, spinning off the platelets

of everything I've made, tiny red planets
in a universe that refuses to stop expanding. *Stop*

is the little sound my heels make unsticking
in the gold mud. No stopping. Just

the progress of the shining migraine. Just
my hand emptying itself of all its coins.

Native

(Crucifixion)

Behind my lost one's head something flickers,
flickers: the light little birds of dismay. Who must
be born breathing grief's cadmium. Born
flying its chemical glare. I am just
an astronaut here, wearing the gravity suit.
But could I learn to eat the toxic light,
wear nothing but the sulfuric clothing that would give
my skin away, put on grace's poison
wings that would let me hover, let me stay?

Deposition

Its emptied weight an unbearable fact
you must in fact bear with your muscles first

(other kinds of bearing come later).
One thing to do now: undo

the sharp things, the mind's metals, whatever
pinned it to the simple shape you'd hung it on.

Steady yourself on the ladder, brace with your arms
and legs when you take love down.

V. Reverse, Crowning Panels

Ten Ways

*(The Resurrected Christ Appears to His Disciples
Behind Locked Doors)*

1.
Thief   what has he stolen   himself   where can
we hide it   we can't fence his
stolen goods.

2.
You're like something brought back
from an archeological dig and everyone
says, *hmmm, beautiful, but what's
it for?* What do we do with you, now
that you're here, a gold statue nobody
wants to melt down but we need
the money more than you can know.

3.
How impassable I'd thought myself,
how densely built, but he runs straight
through me, a string of gold *x*'s
through an empty equation, my hands
as open as vowels.

4.
You come back here like a dog looking
for a lost bone   trying to lick the
last scrap of light off the earth itself   don't you
have enough now.

5.
Fly buzzing in my dream I keep trying
to brush it away but then a bird is
saying *here it is here it is here it is.*

6.

Why did I never notice before you were always
like this always just back from the farthest coast
of light always just settling the clattering wings
always just unlocking the doors and walking
through them all at once always I had
the chance to stand still and say *of course.*

7.

You'd think I'd be more than satisfied, watching you fill
the house like a roman candle with who knows how long
a fuse. But no matter how freely you offer your full
plate of light, you've set off again all the alarms of hunger
for something I never thought I stood a chance getting:
more of the same. Your fault, of course, for bringing
love back practically whole from the deep
well I had to drop it in, hearing
my heart splinter, I thought, along with it.

8.

No telling what might happen now he's opened
a hole in the center of things   I am never
not falling   I can't hear   maybe he can
what this ever downward sounds like   is it like glass giving
way or like water poured slowly into more water

9.

You are pure arrival, pure loss, like a language
I don't know and you the last speaker
and there's never been an alphabet for it, ever.
At some point when I wasn't listening, you must
have said: *put nothing in writing, leave no tracks.*
But oh I want the useless receipt for what I've
spent, everything, on you turning now
into glitter on water before my eyes.

10.

Look at you, a shiny thorn in time's side,
gaudy, exhausting: your tasteless,
expensive gifts. I never said I wanted

to put my hand in the ceaseless
stream of human trespass and reverse
it; never wanted to crouch down and mend
the spectacularly, grossly broken.
I thought time was a solid gold
arrow, pointing always toward the same
nothing much. But here you come spinning
a little gilded weathervane, as light and pretty
as the idea I can't shake of following its directions
no matter where.

Past It

(Thomas in Doubt)

What I'd always imagined was a bright,
permanent elsewhere, or else a kind of winnowing—
body gone transparent, cells spinning
like sparks off a collapsing star. Light,
what else? And here you come, with your open
wounds, showing off your feet, your filthy
hands, telling me: *here it is, can you see
it, the new life.* How can it be, this broken,
stubborn love? I'll never get past it, ever,
the body of this world. I put my hand
right in the dense equation of this moment
and I see the string of numbers does not end.
Bruised star, broken light, it never
finishes disappearing, does it, does it?

Do Me a Favor

(Christ Appears to His Apostles on Lake Tiberias)

Recurring dream   counterfeit dollar
you know I shouldn't be walking here
on nothing but the bright transparency of what I wish.

Do me a favor   don't give me anything else.
Don't load up the nets with what
I'll just have to give away again.

Go so I know I've lost something.
      You never have.
Go so I know there's an ending.
      There never is.
Go so I know water will drown me.
      It may not.
Go so I know.
      You can't.

Lodging

(Christ's Appearance on the Mountain)

I hit the X
the buried jewel
exploding in the
middle of my life.
I'd always known
it was there yet what
a surprise to become
its gold shrapnel
riding away from myself
in every direction
and lodging at last in the
world's itinerant flesh.

VI. Front, Crowning Panel (Lost)

Assumption

Bracelets clatter off.   Gold crown
rolls into zero. The baby falls forever.
To strip ourselves of the imaginary royalty of the world.

Throw you a bone, trace mineral of my disappearance:
undeveloped film unspooled in your hand.
What is the picture: *desire without objects.*

Notes

Catherine Cycle title page: On Catherine's life: Suzanne Noffke, *Catherine of Siena* (Collegeville, MN: Liturgical Press, 1996). On Giovanni di Paolo's paintings: Carl Brandon Strehlke, "The Saint Catherine of Siena Series," in Keith Christiansen, Laurence B. Kanter, and Carl Brandon Strehlke, *Painting in Renaissance Siena* (New York: Metropolitan Museum of Art, 1988).

"Mysterious Communion": I am indebted to the astronomer Martin Rees's description of what an observer viewing an astronaut entering a black hole would see: "An external observer would never witness the astronaut's final fate: any clock would appear to run slower and slower as it fell inward, so the astronaut would appear impaled at the horizon, frozen in time" (*Before the Beginning: Our Universe and Others* [Cambridge, MA: Perseus, 1997]).

"Exchange": Quotation in epigraph is from Jacobus de Voragine, *The Golden Legend: Readings on the Saints*, Vol. II, tr. William Granger Ryan (Princeton UP, 1993).

"Dictation": "*Sounds   who hears them*": adapted from Bassui Tokusho, "The Talk on One Mind" and "Letters to the Zen Priest Iguchi" in Philip Kapleau, *The Three Pillars of Zen* (New York: Doubleday, 1980). "pristine hydrogen": "Pristine hydrogen is transmuted, inside stars, into the basic building blocks of life—carbon, oxygen, iron" (Rees, *Before the Beginning*).

"Her Mother": "the five kinds of tears including fire": adapted from Catherine of Siena, *The Dialogue* (New York: Paulist Press, 1980).

"With the Pope and the College of Cardinals": Epigraphs are from Raymond of Capua's life of Catherine. The first is quoted in George Kaftal, *St. Catherine in Tuscan Painting* (Oxford: Blackfriars, 1949). The second is quoted in Suzanne Noffke's Introduction to Catherine's *Dialogue*. "*Open the ear of your desire*": from Catherine's *Dialogue*.

Stubborn title page: Peter Seiler, "Duccio's *Maestà*: The Function of the Scenes from the Life of Christ on the Reverse of the Altarpiece: A New Hypothesis," *Italian Panel Painting of the Duecento and Trecento*, ed. Victor M. Schmidt (New Haven: Yale UP, 2002).

"Apostles' Dream II": Epigraph from *The Complete Gospels*, ed. Robert J. Miller (New York: HarperCollins, 1994).

"Native": "To come down by a movement in which gravity plays no part. . . . Gravity makes things come down, wings make them rise: What wings raised to the second power can make things come down without weight?" (Simone Weil, *Gravity and Grace*, tr. Arthur Wills [Lincoln: U Nebraska P, 1997]).

"Assumption": Quotations in italics are from Simone Weil, *Gravity and Grace*.